CONTENTS

SUMMARY:

THE CHANGING WORLD ORDER

An Upgraded Brain Series © 2021

This document is geared towards providing exact and reliable information in regards to the topic and issue covered. The publication is sold with the idea that the publisher is not required to render accounting, officially permitted, or otherwise, qualified services. If advice is necessary, legal or professional, a practiced individual in the profession should be ordered.

From a Declaration of Principles which was accepted and approved equally by a Committee of the American Bar Association and a Committee of Publishers and Associations. In no way is it legal to reproduce, duplicate, or transmit any part of this document in either electronic means or in printed format. Recording of this publication is strictly prohibited and any storage of this document is not allowed unless with written permission from the publisher. All rights reserved.

The information provided herein is stated to be truthful and consistent, in that any liability, in terms of inattention or otherwise, by any usage or abuse of any policies, processes, or directions contained within is the solitary and utter responsibility of the recipient reader. Under no circumstances will any legal responsibility or blame be held against the publisher for any reparation, damages, or monetary loss due to the information herein, either directly or indirectly. Respective authors own all copyrights not held by the publisher.

The information herein is offered for information purposes solely, and is universal as so. The presentation of the information is without contract or any type of guarantee assurance.

The trademarks that are used are without any consent, and the publication of the trademark is without permission or backing by the trademark owner. All trademarks and brands within this book are for clarifying purposes only and are owned by the owners themselves, not affiliated with this document.

Disclaimer and Terms of Use: The Author and Publisher has strived to be as accurate and complete as possible in the creation of this book, notwithstanding the fact that he does not warrant or represent at any time that the contents within are accurate due to the rapidly changing nature of the Internet. While all attempts have been made to verify information provided in this publication, the Author and Publisher assumes no responsibility for errors, omissions, or contrary interpretation of the subject matter herein. Any perceived slights of specific persons, peoples, or organizations are unintentional. In practical advice books, like anything else in life, there are no guarantees of results. Readers are cautioned to rely on their own judgment about their individual circumstances and act accordingly. This book is not intended for use as a source of legal, medical, business, accounting or financial advice. All readers are advised to seek services of competent professionals in the legal, medical, business, accounting, and finance fields.

INTRODUCTION

The times ahead will be very different from what we have experienced. We will experience big challenges and changes in the coming years. A changing world order.

I have studied the big history which has led me to this conclusion.

We'll first look at the simplified pattern of the rise and declines of empires.

Then we'll look at them on an individual level.

1: THE BIG PICTURE IN A TINY NUTSHELL

I studied the rise and fall of the last three reserve currency empires (Dutch, British, USA) and six other big empires (Germany, France, Russia, India, Japan, and China) over the last 500 years.

Most of the turbulent times have been because of money and credit collapses, wealth gaps, fights over wealth and power, as well as severe acts of nature which includes epidemics.

Most cycles in history happened for basically the same reasons.

Human productivity is the single most important force in causing the world's total wealth, power and living standards to improve over the long run since we learn to do things better.

For example, the invention of the printing press in Europe increased the knowledge and education available to a lot of people which led to the European Renaissance, the Scientific Revolution, the Enlightenment, and the Industrial Revolution.

Humanity's ability to adapt and improve is the greatest power that produces the long run improvements in our living standard.

Better educated people produce societies that are more innovative, competitive, and productive.

Learning shifted wealth and power away from an agrarian economy where land ownership was the primary source of power to an industrial economy where capitalists that owned production capabilities had power.

Now the shift is happening again but into digital things like data and information processing.

This will become the most valuable thing and this will create conflict over who gets the data. This will be used to gain wealth and power.

The Shift In Power Between Countries

China was the most powerful in the last 1400 years, consistently outperforming Europe in trade.

China entered a steep decline starting from the 1800s.

The Netherlands became one of the world's great empires in the 1600s.

Then it was the UK with power peaking in the 1800s.

Finally came the US which has been the world's superpower for the last 150 years.

Now the US is in relative decline while China is catching up again.

Measures Of Wealth And Power

The primary measures of wealth and power are:

- Education
- Competitiveness
- Technology
- Economic Output
- Share of World Trade
- Military Strength
- Financial Center Strength
- Reserve currency

The Big Cycle

The rise and fall of empires happens broadly in 3 phases:

1. The Ascent Phase

This is characterized by strong leadership, military, education, productivity, financial markets, and general competitive advantages.

There are low levels of debt, small wealth gaps, and a

peaceful world order.

2. The Top Phase

At this stage, there's sustained strength but the seeds of loss in competitive advantages are planted. The rich naturally work less hard, become leisurely, less productive, and seek more luxuries.

An early sign of this phase is when the richest get into debt by borrowing from the poorest. The US did this with China and the British with its poorer colonies.

3. The Decline Phase

The seeds of decline planted during the top phase occur as most or all measures of wealth and power start to reverse.

Debts and the wealth disparity at this stage become very large. There are large gaps in values and politics as people struggle to work well together which lead to political extremism.

The rise of a powerful rival leads to a period of painful fighting, destruction and then a reset that establishes a new world order.

2: THE BIG CYCLE OF MONEY, CREDIT, DEBT, AND ECONOMIC ACTIVITY

Money and credit is the biggest driver of politics and the big cycle. As such, it's important to get an understanding of money and credit.

The Timeless And Universal Fundamentals Of Money And Credit

People, companies, and governments all deal with the same fundamental financial realities.

This is represented by the money that comes in (revenue) and money that goes out (expenses). The net result is their net income. There's the balance sheet which shows assets and liabilities.

The dynamic relationship between income, expenses and savings between individuals, companies, and countries act as the biggest driver of changes in the world order.

One person's cut in expenses will not just hurt that person but many others that depend on that spending to earn their money. This produces a self-reinforcing spiral effect when there's debt involved.

Money, credit, debt and economic activity are inherently cyclical. During the credit creation phase, demand for goods, services, and investments are strong and there's a stimulative effect. When they need to be paid back, everything goes into reverse.

The issue right now is that many entities and governments have low incomes relative to their expenses, and there are big liabilities in pension, healthcare and insurance, relative to their assets.

What Is Money?

Money is a medium of exchange and also a storehold of wealth.

Money and credit has no intrinsic value. They are just pluses and minuses on an accounting system that's designed to allocate resources efficiently to improve productivity. This system breaks down from time to time.

Since the beginning of time, all currencies have been destroyed or devalued.

Reserve Currencies

Governments can print money but they're not of equal value.

The currencies that are most widely accepted around the world are called reserve currencies.

The US dollar is currently the world's dominant

reserve currency which accounts for 55% of all international transactions. A much less important currency is the Euro which accounts for 25% of international transactions. The Japanese Yen, Chinese Renminbi, and the British pound are relatively small reserve currencies for now.

The benefit of having a reserve currency is that the country can borrow a lot more than it otherwise could as well as print money to spend as it sees fit. This is what the US is currently doing. Having a reserve currency is the most important power, even more so than military power. Countries that don't have reserve currencies can find themselves in need of reserve currencies when they have a lot of debt denominated in reserve currencies which they can't print.

The Fundamentals

Money and credit are not wealth. One cannot create more wealth simply by creating more money and credit. To create more wealth, you need more productivity.

If you own a house and the government prints a lot of money and your house goes up in price, you still own the same house. Your actual wealth hasn't increased, only your calculated wealth.

There's a real economy and a financial economy. They're both related and different. Each has its own supply and demand factors. Sometimes lending fuels increases in economic demand and other times into inflation-hedge assets which can cause the currency to decline.

Using market values to measure wealth gives an illusion of changes in wealth that don't really exist.

The Long-Term Debt Cycle

1. Hard Money

Societies usually started with things that had intrinsic value like gold, silver and copper. There's a saying that "gold is the only financial asset that isn't someone else's liability." Gold could be used as both a safe medium of exchange and a safe storehold of wealth.

2. Paper Money

Carrying a lot of metal money was risky and inconvenient so credible parties put the hard money in safe places and then issues paper claims on it. These paper claims on money started becoming money themselves.

3. Increase Debt

These paper claims eventually gets lent out over and over again in exchange for interest payments which creates a boom. Everyone likes it because it leads to rising production and asset prices. While debt is constantly growing, the amount of goods and services stays limited by the amount we can actually produce. The same goes for paper claims on hard money as there's a finite amount of gold on deposit. Trouble inevitably approaches as debts spiral out of control.

4. The Debt Crises

Bank runs start happening. This is where the demand for money is greater than what the bank can provide.

In the case of central banks, if the debt is denominated in a currency that they can print, they'll do that and devalue debt claims. Otherwise, they too will default.

5. Fiat Money

Eventually, claims on money becomes too painful, so governments will abandon them altogether in favor of just "paper money" so the government can print without limit. The government will no longer need to keep any hard money on reserve. The central bankers will print money and debt without restraint until they run out their ability to stimulate credit and economic growth.

Eventually a debt default or devaluation of money occurs.

6. The Return of Hard Money

The overprinting leads to the selling of debt assets and people start fleeing out of the currency and the national debt. People need alternative stores of wealth and that typically means going into gold, other currencies, assets in other countries not having problems and shares that have kept value.

During this period of contraction, there is often fighting within countries as well as between countries over wealth and power.

The government is then forced to go back to some form of hard currency to regain people's trust in the value of money so that credit growth can restart.

Eventually it starts all over again with a restructuring of debts, the monetary system, the domestic order and the international order. The world order, in other words.

America Currently

The new world order began at the end of World War II in 1945 with the US dollar being the world's leading reserve currency. This happened because the US had two-thirds of the world's gold, accounted for half of the world's economic production and was the most dominant military power.

The US dollar was a claim on hard money where the dollar could be exchanged for gold at a fixed price. Eventually, this system broke down when President Nixon defaulted on the US promise to allow holders of the dollar into gold in 1971. This move into fiat money allowed the Federal Reserve to print without restriction.

Since then, there has been massive scale money and

credit creation. Some of this was to ease economic downturns. However, since 2008 there was a shift into debt monetization which includes the printing of money and the direct purchase of financial assets with interest rate policy no longer being effective at around 0%.

Once the pandemic arrived, the US central bank started making direct payments from the government to its citizens as traditional monetary policy became less effective. This is similar to what happened in the early 1930s.

3: THE CHANGING VALUE OF MONEY

The Easy Way Out

There are four ways that the government can deal with a debt crisis:

-Austerity
-Debt default and restructuring
-Transfers of money from the haves to the have nots or redistribution of wealth
-Printing and devaluing money

Policy makers will ultimately end up with money printing because the rest are too painful or difficult to implement. This is what's happening at the moment.

Currencies

People pay too much attention to asset risk and not enough to currency risk.

From 750 currencies that have existed since 1700, only 20% have remained and all of the 20% have been devalued.

The goal of mass money printing is to deal with debt pain. More money printing and credit means reducing the value of debt which hurts holders of debt but it provides relief to people that owe money so that they can put money into the economy.

The issue with this is that it damages the future return of cash and that drives people to flee that currency and its associated debt assets into inflation-hedge assets and other currencies which leads to a fall in the currency.

The bigger currency devaluations have happened in

spurts rather than in a straight line. For example, there was a large US devaluation to finance the Civil War debts in the 1860s. After World War II, the value of money and debt was completely wiped out for the losing countries such as Germany, Japan and Italy, and severely devalued for Great Britain and France.

History shows that there is a big risk in holding cash as a storehold for wealth late in the debt cycles.
Since 2000, there has been a gradual loss in the value of currencies relative to gold.

4: THE BIG CYCLES OF THE DUTCH AND BRITISH EMPIRES

The Big Cycle Of An Empire

Upon the creation of the new world order, there's a peaceful and prosperous period.

People think it will continue to be prosperous so they borrow money to bet on that which leads to a bubble.

The prosperity leads to a wealth gap and the bubble bursts.

Then comes money printing and internal conflict

which leads to wealth redistribution.

Late in the cycle, the rival power becomes more powerful and with bad economic conditions, disagreements between the powers lead to war.

The winners get together to form a new world order.

The US is currently the most powerful empire ()though not by much), it is in relative decline, and China is rising rapidly with no other powers close.

The Last 500 Years

The Dutch Empire

The Dutch was initially under the control of the Spanish empire. The Dutch became powerful enough in 1581 to overthrow them and went on to become the world's richest empire from 1625 until their collapse in 1780. Their peak was around 1650 which was called the Dutch Golden Age.

The Dutch were very educated people that were inventive and the two most important inventions they came up with was ships and capitalism.

The ships were important because it could take around the world with military skills they had obtained from all the fighting that they did in Europe.

The Dutch invented public debt and equity markets where people could collectively lend money and buy ownership in for profit enterprise. They created the first listed company in the world called the Dutch East India Company and the first stock exchange in 1602. All of the financial innovations they created attracted investors and led Amsterdam to become the world financial center.

The Dutch guilder was also the first world reserve currency that wasn't gold and silver because they were the first empire to stretch around the globe and have their currency be widely accepted.

The Dutch empire eventually became more costly to maintain and less competitive. Other countries started to grow in power, especially the British with whom they had increasing clashes over economic issues.

This culminated in the Fourth Anglo-Dutch War which lasted from 1780 until 1784. The British won decidedly on a financial and military basis. This bankrupted the Dutch and caused the collapse of the Dutch empire as well as its debt and equities.

Afterwards, the British and its allies continued to fight others in war including the French which it would win in 1815.

The British Empire

After the war, the winning powers met in a meeting named the Congress of Vienna to decide on the new world order.

This was the start of the British 100 year so called Imperial Century where the British pound became the world's reserve currency and dominant world power.

Global peace and prosperity followed since there was no real challenger to British power.

The British mixture of capitalism, inventiveness and strong global military capability enabled a small country of well educated people to become extremely wealthy and powerful.

The British East India Company replaced the Dutch Easy India Company as the world's most dominant company and London replaced Amsterdam as the world financial center.

During this period of relative global peace and prosperity, the United States grew rapidly to become a leading world power. In the meantime the British empire became more decadent and expensive to maintain as its relative power declined and it borrowed excessively.

The American Empire

The US became an equal power to the British empire around 1900.

After World War 1, the US maintained its isolationism while Britain expanded its global empire.

The debts and wealth gaps built up during the 1920s

which burst in 1929. This led to money printing, the Great Depression, the devaluation of currencies and conflicts over wealth and power.

This culminated in World War II which was won by the winning powers with new technologies including the nuclear bomb.

The US had at this time two thirds of the world's gold and was more powerful economically and militarily than any country in the world. It took on the role of global leadership.

The currencies and debts of the losing powers were wiped out while Britain was left heavily in debt and facing the fall of its empire.

New York became the world's financial center which heralded the beginning of the new world order that has lasted up until today.

5. THE BIG CYCLE OF THE US AND THE DOLLAR. PART 1

The American Start

The history of the US as a nation begins with the colonists that revolted against the British Empire for independence in 1776.

The seeds of innovation was planted in the early 1800s through education and later in technology and competition. This enabled the US to achieve huge amounts of productivity growth starting from around 1870 that led to the US eventually becoming the dominant world power.

1930 To 1939/41: The Economic War

In 1929, the bubble burst with the Great Depression. This led to virtually all countries having major internal conflicts over wealth. Some countries turned populist, autocratic, and nationalistic. The depression turned already bad situations into desperate ones for many countries including Germany, Japan, the Soviet Union, and China.

Franklin D. Roosevelt became president in 1932. He was considered to be a leftist populist. He defaulted on the promise of US dollar convertibility to gold, devalued the US dollar against other currencies and implemented large fiscal spending measures with debt that the Fed Reserve monetized. His 1935 tax bill was commonly referred to as the "Soak the Rich Tax."

Power rather than law dictate international relationships and a series of power struggles ultimately culminated in war and then peace in 1945.

As a principle, there's generally an economic war first before there's a shooting war. This occurred 10 years before World War II with the start of the Great Depression.

The US turned protectionist to keep jobs safe and raised tariffs. Measures employed during economic warfare include asset seizures, blocking capital market access, and blockades.

Countries tend to become autocratic and populist during times of extreme economic pressure because people wants someone strong to bring order amid chaos.

The depression hit Germany especially hard where it incurred huge amounts of bankruptcies and large scale poverty. A battle between populists of the left and right then emerged with Hitler ultimately winning the fight.

1939 To 1945: The Hot War

The US entered the war after the Pearl Harbor attack.

Countries during war will shift from profit making to war making with the government taking control on almost everything including what's being produced, what can be purchased, prices, wages, profits and general access to financial assets.

Protecting one's wealth during war is difficult since capital access is curtailed (stock markets were oftentimes closed), high taxes are placed and the priority is redistributing wealth for the war machine.

World War II was extremely costly in terms of both lives and money with 40-75 million people killed and $4-7 trillion dollars in inflation-adjusted terms.

The US came out as the major winner since most of the fighting happened outside of US land and the US lent a lot of money to Allied powers.

6. THE BIG CYCLE OF THE US AND THE DOLLAR. PART 2

The Post-War Geopolitical And Military System

After World War II, the big three winning powers, namely the US, Britain and the Soviet Union, created the new world order.

The world was split into the US-led countries of capitalism and democracy, and the Soviet-led countries of communism and autocracy.

The US world included over 40 countries which adopted the US monetary system and this has continued on until today.

Relationship between countries is like operating in the jungle. Raw power is what matters most which is why a strong military is important. Both American and the Soviet Union invested an enormous amount in nuclear weapons for deterrence.

Military alliances were formed according to ideological lines including the North Atlantic Treaty Organization (NATO) in 1949 and the Southeast Asia Treaty Organization in 1954, and the Soviet military alliance in 1955 built the Warsaw Pact.

The Post-War Monetary And Economic Systems

Money between countries and within countries are very different. A country can force its population to use paper money that the government prints. However, the rules are different for transactions between countries since money needs to be acceptable to both countries. This is why countries have gold and reserve currencies to facilitate international transactions.

Governments have restricted people's ability to own or transact in gold because gold cannot be controlled by the government and it therefore represents a threat to the system as people would have an alternative to government mandated money.

The Bretton Woods Agreement was made in Bretton Woods, New Hampshire in 1944 which made the US dollar the world's primary reserve currency. The Soviet Union also created its own monetary system around the ruble but it was a much less significant.

Following World War II, the US became incredibly rich as it amassed two-thirds of the world's money while most other countries were broke.

The US entered a long period of peace and prosperity with the new world order and no challenger in sight.

The Late-1960S Weakening Fundamentals That Led To The End Of The Bretton Woods Monetary System

In the 1960s, Americans were spending a lot on consumption as trade balances worsened with the US spending more than it was earning.

The US was spending a lot on the Vietnam War as well as on domestic social programs.

Eventually on August 15, 1971, the Bretton Woods monetary system broke down as President Nixon broke the US promise on its dollar convertibility into gold.

The Inflationary And Troubled Seventies

The US dollar went on to tumble in value on international markets.

The new monetary fiat monetary system was no longer linked to gold and the constraint now taken off, there was a huge increase in money and credit as well as in inflation.

Panic led people out of the dollar and a drive into real

estate, gold and collectibles from 1971 to 1981.

The 1979-82 Move To Tight Money And Conservatism

In August 1979, Paul Volcker, the head of the Federal Reserve, tightened money to break the back of inflation.

This drove the world economy into the worst recession since the Great Depression and ultimately cost President Carter his presidency.

In reaction to the nose diving economy and stock market, the Federal Reserve slowly cut interest rates.

The Disinflationary And Booming Eighties

The falling inflation and interest rates in the 1980s saw the US stock market and economy come back full throttle.

Emerging economies that had a lot of US dollar debt on the other hand suffered from inflationary depressions as they weren't able to print their way out of trouble.

This period demonstrated the benefits of having the world's debts and money denominated in US dollars.

1990-2008: Globalizing, Digitalizing, And Booming Financed By Debt

The 1990-2000 period marked the Soviet Union's decline, China's rise, globalization, technology, and increasing wealth gaps.

Middle-class workers in the US became increasingly replaced by labor in China and other countries and through technology.

There have been a few economic cycles since the 1990s including the dot-com bubble, the 2008 global financial crisis, and the 2020 pandemic crisis.

The 2008-20 Money-Financed Capitalist Boom Period

The 2008 Global Financial Crisis led central banks to exhaust interest rate driven monetary policy with interest rates lowered down to 0%.

To effectively stimulate the economy, central banks went on to printing lots of money and purchasing financial assets directly. This caused financial asset prices to increase and it was beneficial to those that owned financial assets.

This caused wealth and income gaps to widen. The gaps are currently the widest it has been since the 1930-45 period with deep political divisions.

The US, under President Trump, has been intensifying conflicts with China over areas of trade, technology, geopolitics, and capital.

In March 2020, with the nosedive in economic activity as a result of the pandemic, the Federal Reserve printed a lot of money to give to people and companies.

Where America Is In Its Big Cycle

Looking at the statistics, it would seem that the US is at around 75% in the cycle.

Reversing declines is hard because a lot of the damage has already been done.

Having said that, if we can earn more than we spend, work hard and smart, and make the system work for the majority of the people, then we might be able to do it.

7. THE BIG CYCLE OF CHINA AND ITS CURRENCY

I have gotten to know Chinese people from the lowest to the highest in rank in a very intimate way over the past 36 years.

The loyalties and media distortions has stood in the way of thoughtfully exploring differing perspectives.

A Brief History Of China

Any attempt to understand China means understanding some of its 4,000 year history and the many patterns that have repeated in it. Its history is not only very ancient but also particularly well documented.

China's highly civilized societies began 4,000 years ago with many dynasties.

The Xia Dynasty started from 2000 BC, lasted for 400 years and was highly civilized and created the Bronze Age.

Another includes the Qin Dynasty which united most of what we call China for the first time in 221 BC.

During the Tang Dynasty from the 900s to 1200, China was the most innovative and dynamic economy in the world.

Most of the last 1,400 years of dynasties were powerful, civilized, and cultured.

From the early 1800s until the 1900s, China lost its power while Europe gained theirs. This shift of wealth and power where China was uniquely weak should be considered an anomaly rather than the norm.

A Chinese Perspective

Americans tend to fight for what they want in the present, China strategizes on how to get what they want in the future.

Chinese leaders tend to read philosophy, how reality works and you can see this expressed in their writings and speeches.
Though intensive studies of their longer history, the Chinese are more interested in a longer time horizon instead of just getting quick wins. They're more focused on strategy than on tactic.

Chinese leaders will make plans, implement and then set out clear metrics to judge their performance.

China's Lessons And Its
Ways Of Operating

The dominant philosophies of the Chinese has been of Confucianism, Taoism, Legalist before Marxism and capitalism got added.

Confucianism values harmony, widespread education, and meritocracy. People know their roles in the hierarchy and respects and obeys those above them.

Legalism believes in a strong, harsh government and is akin to fascism.

Taoism is about seeking harmony from balancing opposites – the yin and the yang.

Confucianism has been the most dominant through time. The Chinese put the family and the collective first whereas Americans put the individual first. You can think of the Chinese government as being run from the top down like a family for the collective while America is run from the bottom up for the individual.

Since the beginning of recorded history, Chinese systems have been hierarchical and non-egalitarian. There has been a general emphasis on knowing one's place and playing that role.

The Decline From 1800 Until 1949

The Qing dynasty, which was the last of the Chinese dynasties, became weak and decadent. The financial system collapsed under debts that couldn't be paid while there was civil war and a rebellion raging.

The British empire and other Western countries continued to become stronger and they took increasing control of China as the Qing government tried unsuccessfully to fight them off.

The British smuggled opium into China in order to get China to trade. This led to the First Opium War in which the British Navy defeated China and took control of China's main ports including Shanghai, Canton, and Hong Kong.

In addition to the Opium Wars, the Qing government borrowed heavily from foreigners to combat internal rebellions including the Boxer Rebellion.

These factors in addition to acts of nature created what came to be known as the Century of Humiliation.

Enter Marxism-Leninism

Karl Marx's most important theory is called dialectical materialism. Dialectical is about how opposites work together to create change and materialism about everything physical.

Dialectical materialism is a way of seeing things unfold and the process of synthesizing contradictions to create progress. For example, the conflict between capitalism and communism.

These forces were at work in China during Mao Zedong's life who had been greatly influenced by Marxism-Leninism. After World War II ended, China then had its own internal war between communists and capitalists which ended in 1949 with a new communist domestic order under Mao.

The Rise From 1949 Until Now

Phase 1, 1949 to 1976: The Mao Phase of Building the Foundation

During this period, he consolidated his power, built China's foundation of governing, kept China closed off from the world and ruled China until his death in 1976.

He followed a strictly communist system whereby the government nationalized businesses and redistributed farmland from landowners to the ones that worked on the farm. Everyone got the same basic pay regardless of whether they worked.

The Soviet Union went from being an ally to an enemy during this period as their respective leaders started criticizing each other openly. This led Mao to open up relations with the US in 1971 to neutralize the Soviet threat. Trade and other exchanges soon followed.

Phase 2, 1978 to 2012: Deng Xiaoping and His Successors Implement Economic Reforms and Opens China Up

Deng Xiaoping became leader at age 74 in 1978. China at this stage was very poor with a per capita income of less than $200 per year.

He saw the blend of communism and capitalism that became referred to as "socialism with Chinese characteristics" as the next phase of development. He believed that these naturally opposing ideologies would work well together to produce progress in China's development.

Lee Kuan Yew of Singapore once said that Deng was the greatest leader of the 20th century because he was a very smart, open-minded learner that advanced China and delivered huge results for its population of about a billion people.

He opened China up to the world, introduced and developed capitalism, and built a symbiotic relationship with the US.

The US would purchase low-priced products from China while the Chinese would lend money so Americans could finance such purchases. This seemed strange given that the Chinese were earning about 1/40 of Americans yet were the ones lending money to finance overconsumption.

After Deng's death, his successors continued on the same path and China grew richer and became an almost comparable power to the US.

In 2008, the global financial crisis led to global tensions over wealth and resentment started building up against China for job losses and against elites that benefited from globalization. With wealth gaps widening, populism and nationalism grew around the world. The US-China relationship started to shift to the point where China's development now came to be viewed as a threat.

During 2009 to 2012, China deployed large fiscal and monetary stimulus to combat economic weakness.

Phase 3, 2012 to now: The Xi Jinping Phase

Xi Jinping came to power in 2012. His administration further reformed and opened up the Chinese economy and markets, managed debt growth, and built technological capabilities.

Since then, China's strength has continued to grow and become more openly assertive while the US has become more confrontational.

Donald Trump was elected as a populist president in 2016 as he tapped into popular resentment. Globalization reversed and conflicts in trade, technology, geopolitics and capital has intensified between the US and China.

In 2018, Xi consolidated his power in the belief that China and the world generally will enter a more challenging phase and that leadership over the next few years will be especially important.

China generally has come very far in the last 40 years. It went from being one of the most backward countries to one of the two most powerful countries in the world in terms of economy, technology, military and geopolitics.

8. US-CHINA RELATIONS AND WARS

In view of the US-China relationship, there ca be a win-win relationship or a lose-lose mutually threatening relationship.

When two competing powers have similar powers, the risks of war are high unless both parties have very high trust that they won't be killed.

Trade And Economic War

The current US-China trade war has not been taken very far.

If one of the countries cut the other off from essential imports (like rare earth elements from China), this would mark a dangerous escalation.

Both countries are decoupling and will become more independent of each other with more focus on domestic production.

Technology War

The winner of the technology war will likely win all other wars so this is the most important war.

The US and China are the main players in the technology industry.

The US currently has the lead in technological capabilities overall although its advantage is diminishing.

China will likely take the lead in technology and adopt the advantages of AI quicker than the US in its decision making process.

The US is limiting Chinese technology and its growing competitiveness by blocking its usage in the US and abroad.

China currently depends on the US (as well as countries the US can influence) for essential imported technology. If the US shuts off access to these technologies, it would also mark a dangerous escalation. In 5-10 years on the other hand, China will be in a stronger position than the US technologically and both countries will be much more technologically decoupled.

Geopolitical War

The Century of Humiliation and foreign incursions have fueled Chinese desire for sovereignty over the Chinese mainland, Taiwan, Hong Kong, and the East and South China Seas. The Chinese also don't want to be caught in such a vulnerable position where it can be pushed around by foreign powers again.

The biggest issue is Taiwan and whether there will

be a Fourth Taiwan Strait Crisis. While China does not want a military conflict with the US, it also has its red lines that if crossed will lead to war.

Both the US and China will prioritize countries that are geographically close, have essentials like minerals and technology, and, to some degree, export markets.

Over the next 5-10 years, countries will start aligning themselves with either China or the US. It's a question which countries are currently struggling with based on conflicting economic and military considerations.

Capital War

The main risk for China is being cut off from capital while for the US, it's losing its reserve currency status.

The US has the greatest power over the international financial system and can enforce the biggest range of sanctions.

The limit of the US dollar's reserve currency status is currently being tested through massive money printing, the dollar being weaponized through capital controls, negative real returns on the dollar, and having a fiat monetary system.

The US is at risk of losing this power while the Chinese are in a position to gain it.

China's currency and capital markets will develop at a rapid clip over the next 5-10 years to be competitive with the US dollar and US credit markets.

Military War

The next significant war will likely be far worse than what most people think.

The US and China are testing each other militarily in the East and South China Seas. China is stronger in the East and South China Seas while the US is stronger globally.

The rate of Chinese military improvement over the

last 10 years has been rapid and, at this pace, can potentially achieve military dominance in 5-10 years.

Potential flashpoints include Taiwan, the East and South China Seas, and North Korea. Other possibilities include India and Vietnam.

Culture War

How we are with each other is of huge importance, especially when dealing with differences.

Chinese culture takes a top down approach and puts the common interests over individual interests. American culture takes a bottom up approach, favoring individual freedom over collective interests.

The cultural differences are deeply rooted and one cannot expect either side to give up their values and their system.

The American and Chinese systems are different because of differences in history and circumstances that produced these cultures. Both sides can choose to accept, tolerate, and respect each other's right to do as each thinks best.

The War With Ourselves: The Enemy Is Us

The most important war we now face is with ourselves.

We control how strong or weak we become. We know the factors that enable countries to rise and maintain their great strength.

The internal challenges we face in the form of domestic political wars, the factional wars, the war against climate change, and so on, is our biggest battle.

These are all within our control and we can change course to make sure we're going the right way.

Deserve Victory! - Winston Churchill

9. INTERNAL ORDER AND DISORDER

The US is currently at an important point in time where tensions can potentially lead to a revolution or a civil war, or both.

These periods typically happen once in a lifetime and the swing from great to terrible times might seem hard to imagine right now. But these swings have been the norm in history.

The Timeless Universal Forces That Changes The Internal Order

1. The Wealth and Power Class Struggle

A very small percentage of population have generally controlled most of the wealth and power throughout history.

Wealthy people own the means of wealth production and work together with those in power in order to maintain it.

2. The Balance of Power Dynamic

When you have two competing powers that can destroy each other, the risk of a deathly fight is high.

The dynamics of forming allies and enemies, and having wars usually follow this pattern:

i. Formation of alliances on opposite sides with generally equal power
ii. The two sides struggle until a winner is determined
iii. Those on the winning side fight among themselves for control until one of them becomes dominant and consolidates power
iv. With only one country firmly in power and no one willing to challenge that power, there follows peace and prosperity that produces wealth and power inequalities.

v. The inequalities widen until the dominant power weakens and a new struggle occurs leading to this whole process repeating over again.

3. Short-Term Over Long-Term

People generally prefer short-term rewards over long-term wellbeing which drives the overarching cycles.

This is especially true of governments but applies at all levels from individuals to companies.

We can expect governments to borrow and spend until they can no longer do so by which time there will be a day of reckoning. This usually involves some form of revolutionary restructuring.

4. Failure to Learn From History

Big cycles lasts longer than a lifetime and it is not enough to base decisions only on one's own experiences. We must learn the lessons of history.

What people will likely face will be new for them and not like anything they've experienced before.

10. INTERNAL CYCLES

There are 6 stages that internal orders typically go through and it generally takes around 100 years (give or take many years) to go through them on average.

Stage 1 occurs when there's a new leadership and a new order.

Stage 2 involves setting up systems of resource allocation and government systems.

Stage 3 is a period of peace and prosperity.

Stage 4 sees a build up of excess debt and a widening gap in wealth and politics.

Stage 5 is when this leads to terrible financial conditions and conflict.

Stage 6 is when the country runs out of money and then there is a terrible conflict in the form of a civil war or a revolution.

The US currently appears to be in Stage 5 where it has large deficits, large debts, and wealth gaps. The Federal Reserve is printing a lot of money and buying lots of government debt to finance government spending.

Generally the places that have the biggest wealth gaps, debts and declines in incomes are most likely to have conflicts.

At some stage, more money will need to be raised or expenditures have to be cut. Since cutting expenses will be too painful, the haves will generally be the ones to foot the bill for debt servicing and reduce deficits through increased taxation.

In the final period of Stage 5, the legal and police systems becomes political weapons by those that control them. There are more violent protests.

On a personal note, if you are in doubt, you should get out while the going is good. When things get bad, people will no longer be able to leave. The same is true for money as countries introduce capital controls during this period.

Nothing is forever except change and evolution.

To handle change well, one must know where in the cycle one is and to understand the principles for dealing with them.

The most important thing now is for us all to work well together to have productive win-win relationships that grows the pie and divides the pie well so that more people can be happy instead of one side dominating another.

SUMMARY

The primary measures of wealth and power are:

- Education
- Competitiveness
- Technology
- Economic Output
- Share of World Trade
- Military Strength
- Financial Center Strength
- Reserve currency

The Big Cycle in Summary:

1. The Ascent Phase

This is characterized by strong leadership, military, education, productivity, financial markets, and general competitive advantages.

There are low levels of debt, small wealth gaps, and a

peaceful world order.

2. The Top Phase

At this stage, there's sustained strength but the seeds of loss in competitive advantages are planted. The rich naturally work less hard, become leisurely, less productive, and seek more luxuries.

An early sign of this phase is when the richest get into debt by borrowing from the poorest. The US did this with China and the British with its poorer colonies.

3. The Decline Phase

The seeds of decline planted during the top phase occur as most or all measures of wealth and power start to reverse.